Dinosaur Mums
and Babies

by Leonie Bennett

Consultant: Dougal Dixon

D1380122

ALIS

2629107

ABERDEENSHIRE LIBRARY AND	
INFORMATION SERVICES	
2629107	
HJ	697198
J567.9	£3.99
JU	JNF

CONTENTS

Words in **bold** are explained in the glossary.

Dinosaur eggs

Dinosaurs laid eggs.

Some dinosaur eggs were **oval**.

Troodon eggs were oval.

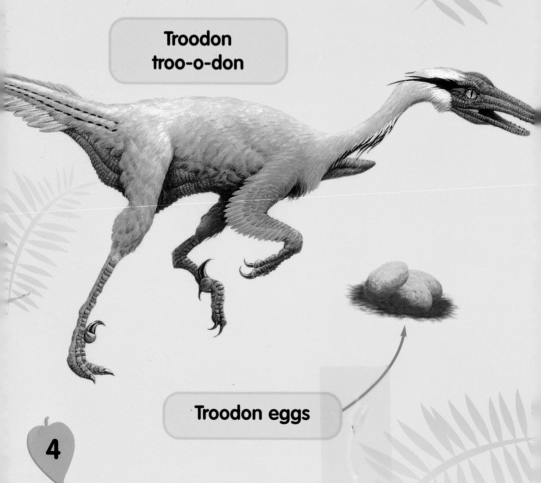

Troodon
troo-o-don

Troodon eggs

Therizinosaur
ther-ee-zine-o-sor

Some dinosaur
eggs were round.

This dinosaur's eggs
were round.

Therizinosaur
egg

How big were dinosaur eggs?

Some eggs were bigger
than a football.

Some eggs were
smaller than a golf ball.

6

The biggest dinosaur egg we know belongs to this dinosaur. It was about 30 centimetres long.

Hypselosaurus
hip-sel-o-sor-us

Where did dinosaurs lay their eggs?

Some dinosaurs laid their eggs in nests on the ground.

Eggs

This animal lived in the sea.

It came on land to lay its eggs.

It dug a hole and laid its eggs inside.

Plesiosaur
pless-ee-o-sor

Keeping the eggs warm

This dinosaur is sitting on its nest.

It is keeping its eggs warm.

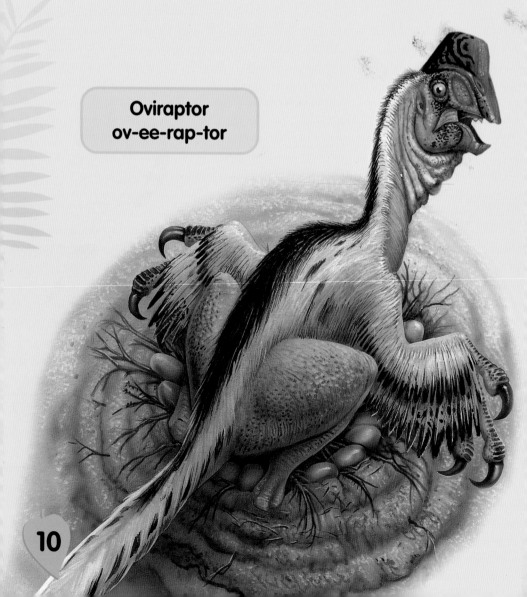

Oviraptor
ov-ee-rap-tor

Big dinosaurs did not sit on their eggs. They would have broken them!

Big dinosaurs hid their eggs in leaves. The leaves kept the eggs safe and warm.

How big were dinosaur babies?

Apatosaurus was one of the biggest dinosaurs. A baby Apatosaurus was as big as a cat.

Apatosaurus
a-pat-o-sor-us

baby   adult

The baby grew very fast. At 15 years old it was almost as big as an adult.

This is a **skeleton** of a baby dinosaur.

It is a baby Mussaurus.

Mussaurus
moo-sor-us

Looking after the babies

Some dinosaurs looked after their babies.

They kept them safe from danger.

Tyrannosaurus rex
tie-ran-o-sor-us rex

14

This Triceratops mother is fighting
a **meat-eater**.

The meat-eater wants to eat her baby.

Triceratops
try-serra-tops

What did dinosaur babies eat?

Some dinosaurs were plant-eaters.

Their babies had to learn to find the plants they liked.

Some dinosaurs were meat-eaters.

Their babies had to learn to hunt.

Special dinosaur mothers

Look at the Maiasaura. Its name means 'good mother lizard'.

It looked after its babies.

This dinosaur mother chewed the leaves of plants to make them soft. Then she gave them to her babies.

Size

Grapefruit   Egg

Maiasaura
my-a-sor-a

19

Babies in the sea

Ichthyosaurus lived in the sea.

It did not lay eggs.

It did not make a nest.

Its babies were born alive.

They were born underwater.

Ichthyosaurus
ick-thee-o-sor-us

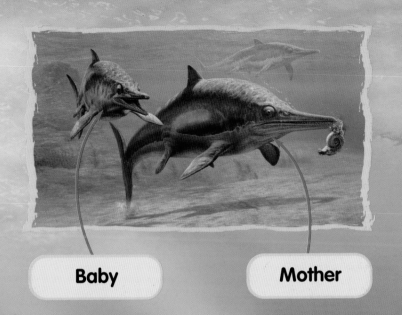

Baby

Mother

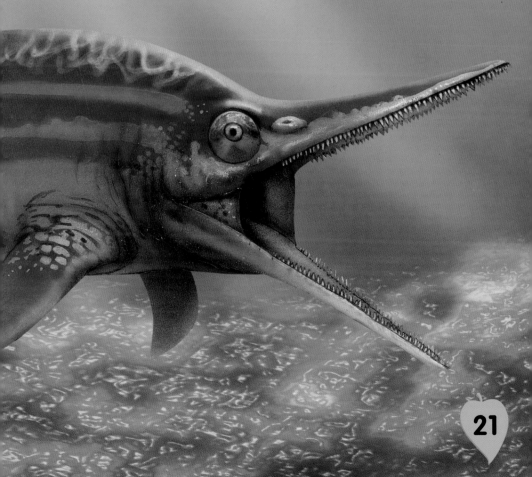

Glossary

Ichthyosaurus
A swimming creature that was around at the time of the dinosaurs.

meat-eater
A dinosaur that ate other animals.

oval
A rounded shape, like a chicken's egg.

skeleton
All the bones inside an animal's body form its skeleton.

Troodon
A small but fast meat-eating dinosaur.

Index

Copyright © ticktock Entertainment Ltd 2008
First published in Great Britain in 2008 by ticktock Media Ltd.,
Unit 2, Orchard Business Centre, North Farm Road, Tunbridge Wells, Kent TN2 3XF
ISBN 978 1 84696 763 4 pbk
Printed in China

A CIP catalogue record for this book is available from the British Library. All rights reserved. No part of this publication may be reproduced, copied, stored in a retrieval system or transmitted in any form or by any means electronic, mechanical, photocopying, recording or otherwise without prior written permission of the copyright owner.

We would like to thank: Penny Worms, Shirley Bickler and Suzanne Baker and the National Literacy Trust.

Picture credits (t=top, b=bottom, c=centre, l-left, r=right, OFC= outside front cover)
Simon Mendez: 4c, 8-9, 16 23b; Philip Hood: 1, 4cr, 5l, 5r, 7, 8l, 11b, 11tr, 13b, 17, 19 22b, 23t; Shutterstock: 6c, 6b; Luis Rey: 10l, 20-21, 22t; John Alston: 12, 21t; Corbis: 13tr, 23c; Pulsar EStudio: 14-15.

Every effort has been made to trace the copyright holders, and we apologise in advance for any unintentional omissions. We would be pleased to insert the appropriate acknowledgements in any subsequent edition of this publication.